Y0-EKR-260

THE COOKIE BOOKIE

THE COOKIE BOOKIE

FRUIT COOKIES

SEED NUT COOKIES

SPICE COOKIES

WHOLEGRAIN COOKIES

CHOCOLATE COOKIES

SHORTBREADS

by DIANE FINE AND RIA TEALE

Copyright © 1983 by Diane Fine and Ria Teale

Cover illustration: Diane Fine

Originally published in Canada in 1983 by NC Press Limited

All rights reserved. No part of this book may be reproduced or utilized in
any form or by any means, electronic or mechanical, including photocopy-
ing, recording or by any information storage and retrieval system, without
permission in writing from the Publisher. Inquiries should be addressed
to Permissions Department, William Morrow and Company, Inc., 105
Madison Ave., New York, N.Y. 10016.

Library of Congress Cataloging in Publication Data

Fine, Diane.
  The cookie bookie.

  1. Cookies. I. Teale, Ria. II. Title.
TX772.F55 1985   641.8′654   84-15948
ISBN 0-688-04179-5

Printed in the United States of America

First Quill Edition

1 2 3 4 5 6 7 8 9 10

For Bobby, Jeremy, David and Noah Fine

and

Alan, Emma and Philip Teale

ACKNOWLEDGMENTS

We would like to thank everyone who helped with the preparation of this book—especially our families and friends who conscientiously sampled our efforts morning, noon, and night.

—DIANE AND RIA

Contents

Introduction   11

Helpful Hints   13
Ingredients   16
Tools   20

Seed Cookies   23

Caraway Seed Cookies   25
Open Sesames   27
Poppy Seed Cookies   29
Cardamom Honey Pryanik   31

Nut Cookies   33

Almond Crescents   35
Chinese Almond Cookies   37
Coconut Crunch   39
Hazelnut Cookies   41
Mandelbread   43
Peanut Butter Cookies   45

Pecan Pearls   47
Walnut Rugelach   49

Whole Wheat Cookies   51

Gerard's Buckwheat Inventions   53
Healthy Wealthy Cookies   55
Molasses Flapjacks   57
Muesli Pieces   59
Scottish Oatcakes   61
Bran Hermits   63
Ria's Zig-Zogs   65
Granola Bars   67
Granola Mix   68

Shortbreads   69

Cashew Shortbread   71
Coconut Puffs   73
Coffee-Toffee Shortbread   75
Chocolate Peppermint Shortbread   77
Whole Wheat Shortbread   79

Chocolate Cookies   81

Chocolate Chip Cookies   83
Chocolate Chip Plus   85
Chocolate Mulattoes   87
Chocolate Rice Date Crispies   89
Diane's Dreams   91
Helene's Florentines   93

Spice Cookies   95

Black Pepper Biscuits   97
Curry Biscuits   99
Cinnamon Triangles   101
Ginger Snaps   103
Gingerbread Men   105
Speculaas   107

Fruit Cookies   109

Banana Cookies   111
Currant Cookies   113
Date Cookies   115
Hamantashen   117
Orange Cookies   119
Lime Biscuits   121
Applesauce Cookies   123
Applesauce   124

Introduction

Once upon a time, there was a little Canadian girl and a little Dutch girl who, among other things, had cookies in common. After many months of experimenting and "expanding," they had so many cookies they didn't know what to do. So . . . they decided to share their delectable discoveries with you!

Being wives and mothers, they found that baking cookies offered a creative challenge. Both faced a constant shortage of time and money. (One was even known to devour cookies while still in their frozen state!) The simple, no-fuss preparation of inexpensive, wholesome cookies was ideally suited to their hectic life-styles.

They discovered that the word "cookie" originated from the Dutch word *koekje* meaning small cake. One of the earliest known recipes for such small crisp cakes dates back as far as 1563, in the case of simnel cakes in England. These cakes became popular because they solved the problem of stale leftovers: They were handy and portable and had better keeping qualities. Another early cookie was developed by seafaring people of the 17th century who baked a bread-type biscuit with flour, fat, and water, omitting the rising agents of eggs and yeast to make sure they would keep during their long voyages.

Down through the centuries, little has changed. The advantages still hold true but, with the advance of technology and expertise, cookies can be much more wholesome, varied, and palatable. One no longer has to be a wayfaring seafarer to try the cookies of other lands.

Our two cooks believe in maintaining the home-baked tradition of cookies and the pleasures derived in their preparation. They have discovered it can be just as gratifying to bake the cookies as it is to present and consume them.

Everyone seems to benefit from the therapeutic, tactile involvement of mixing, shaping, pressing, and cutting cookie dough. Diane and Ria find their children especially enjoy participating in the preparation, and the hardy nature of the cookie dough is ideally suited for their less delicate handling. Of course, once involved in the evolution of a cookie, children are much more appreciative of the finished product. The sumptuous aromas that waft through the kitchen are further rewards.

On the practical side, Diane and Ria find that cookies are quicker to prepare than cakes and breads because they seldom require much whipping, kneading, or rising. Every mother's dream is to replace the dreaded chocolate bar in her child's diet with a healthy, nutritious alternative. Homemade cookies are their answer to this problem. Just knowing that they can provide their loved ones with something both salubrious and sweet is incentive enough to embark upon yet another cookie-baking adventure.

Cookies are decorative and most appealing when stored in a variety of glass jars that display them in all their glory. Presentation requires only arranging a selection of cookies on a doily-covered serving plate (impressive to even the most sophisticated guest!), doing away with the need for cutlery and plates.

Another bonus (passed down from those ancient mariners) is the ease of storage. Most cookies can be stored in airtight jars or tins for many weeks (shortbreads being particularly well-known for their longevity). Some cookies are best preserved by freezing them at the height of freshness. This isn't necessarily an inconvenience as they defrost in minutes. Often one can freeze the prebaked dough and bake the cookies when desired. A recipe calling for refrigeration before slicing is ideally suited for freezing.

The following recipes should inspire you to new adventures in the world of home-baked cookies. After all is said and done, the life of a cookie should be brief!

So, if you happen upon a trail of crumbs in the woods, follow it and perhaps you will discover the little Canadian girl and the little Dutch girl, living happily ever after, in their wholegrain gingerbread houses with all their gingerbread men.

Helpful Hints

Conundrums such as "How deep is a spoonful?," "How wide should a cookie pan be?," "How mixed is mixed?," and "How done is done?" have plagued cookie bakers for centuries.

Before we divulge some of the mysteries, we'd like to emphasize (once again) the fact that cookies, unlike most other baked goods, tend to be of a hardy nature and survive most mismanagements in their preparation. Even so, you're bound to find some eccentric family member or friend who just loves dry, bland biscuits, which you can generously serve up as burnt offerings.

If you follow a recipe closely, providing that it is a good recipe with well-proportioned ingredients, chances are the results will be memorable (barring major catastrophes such as dropping a bagful of flour into the mixing bowl, or forgetting that you have put the cookies in the oven over an hour ago). So don't be intimidated by these recipes. Following them should provide you with the opportunity to relax, unwind, and enjoy a delicious snack. Once you get the hang of it, you can create your own masterpieces.

Variations
There are two basic types of doughs: soft doughs, which must be

dropped in spoonfuls or pressed through a cookie mold; and stiff doughs, which can be manipulated and rolled with a rolling pin or your hands and then cut and pressed into shapes with various utensils. Both doughs can produce either a dry, crisp cookie or a moist, chewy one. You cannot necessarily predict the outcome just by the texture of the uncooked dough.

Preparation

If you have an electric oven, always preheat to the desired temperature so that it will be ready for baking when you are.

Grease cookie sheets with unsalted fats—preferably sweet butter. For delicate cookies, line the pan with greased parchment paper; the cookies will peel off easily when slightly cooled.

After reading the recipe from start to finish, arrange all your equipment and ingredients so that they're within easy reach. Also, best results come from using ingredients at room temperature.

Because cookies bake quickly, a timer is advisable.

Systemization

The basic procedure for mixing ingredients is as follows. The oils and sugars are whipped or beaten together so that they become light and fluffy. The eggs, if called for, are added one at a time, followed by the flavorings (extracts, juices, and rinds). Then the dry ingredients, such as flours, rolled oats, chocolate chips, seasonings (spices), nuts, and/or dried fruit are mixed or sifted together just before they are added to the first mixture. All ingredients are blended in just enough to incorporate them well. An overworked dough yields a tough cookie.

Manipulation

Let the dough rest for a few minutes to allow it to mellow. If handling the dough, make sure your hands are cool. Keep a bowl of cold water or flour handy in which to dip your hands when working with a sticky dough. This also applies to the use of cookie cutters and presses.

When rolling out the dough with a rolling pin, make sure to flour lightly the surface upon which you are working, as well as the rolling pin. If the dough is too soft to manage, wrap it in waxed paper or plastic wrap and put it in the refrigerator for about 2 hours (or in the freezer for about 15 minutes) to firm it up.

For soft doughs, place or drop the mounds of dough about 1½" apart on the baking sheet, unless otherwise indicated, to allow for spreading. In this case, when spoonfuls are called for, make sure they are heaped.

The position of the cookie sheet in the oven is important. Place it on the middle rack. Only one rack should be used at a time to ensure even circulation of heat.

Materialization

There are various ways of telling when a cookie is done, apart from following the baking time recommended in the recipe. Remember, that only represents an approximation, due to differences in ovens, altitude, cooking ingredients, and equipment. The most obvious, telltale sign is the euphoric aroma of baked cookies. Don't automatically assume that the cookies must look golden or brown before you take them out: Shortbread cookies that brown are overdone. Dough loses its shininess when cooked; the surface becomes dull.

When cookies are baked, wait a minute before you take them off the pan, to give them a chance to solidify before you disturb them. Then, with a metal spatula, carefully place them onto a wire rack to cool. Make sure you don't place them on top of each other, so that they cool evenly and keep their shape.

Our cookies are so scrumptious we can't bear to throw out a crumb; save all the leftovers in an airtight container for future use in crusts and toppings.

Every type of cookie is different, but with practice you will become a cookie virtuoso, finely tuned to the appliances and ingredients you are working with.

Preservation and Refrigeration

Cookies can be stored in tins, plastic containers, or glass jars. We prefer the latter for aesthetic as well as practical reasons. One never has to worry about cookies going stale when they are displayed attractively and conspicuously. Crisp cookies are best stored in a jar with a loose-fitting lid to preserve freshness. Soft, moist cookies retain their flavor and moisture in containers with tight-fitting lids. Never store different cookies together, especially moist and crisp cookies, as they lose their respective flavors and textures.

To crisp cookies that have become soft, warm them in a 300° oven for five minutes. You can store a slice of orange, lemon, or apple with soft cookies to help keep them moist. (This also enhances their flavor!) Cookies without eggs, such as shortbreads, can last for months; most others have a shelf-life of one to two weeks. All can be stored in the refrigerator for longer; uncooked dough or baked cookies can go into the freezer for up to six months.

Ingredients

Flours

Commercially produced all-purpose white flour, which can be found in any supermarket, works well in all these recipes. White processed flour characteristically has less bulk and produces lighter baked goods than whole wheat flour.

We are partial to the unbleached, soft, whole wheat variety (hard flour is only used for breadbaking), not only because we value its considerable nutritional qualities (the bran coating and germ of the grain are not discarded as they are with white flour) but because we prefer the flavor and texture it produces in baked goods. We use white flour only in recipes where delicate and light results are desired.

Ultimately, the choice of flours rests with the baker. We find that using half white and half whole wheat works well, but any combination of flours can be used.

It is not necessary to sift flour, but if a light cookie is desired, sift the dry ingredients together before folding them carefully into the butter mixture.

When measuring, the flour should not be packed down—just stir lightly and weigh or measure accurately. Too much flour can make cookies heavy and dry. The consistencies and weights of different flours vary slightly, so feel free to adjust their quantities according to the consistency of dough described in the recipes.

Baking Powder/Baking Soda

Baking soda is used in recipes calling for fruit, brown sugar, or sour milk; baking powder is usually used in recipes that do not include fruit. Keep containers of baking powder tightly covered as it loses its gas-producing potency, having a shelf-life of no more than one year.

Oils

Liquid and solid fats may not be substituted for each other when baking, as is often done in other areas of cooking. We recommend corn or safflower liquid oils to bake with, as they have no flavor.

Unsalted butter is a superior and, according to many, a healthier solid-fat product, but a good-quality margarine can be substituted totally or partially to produce a less expensive cookie. Don't forget that the quality of your finished product depends on the quality of ingredients used. (And don't forget to adjust the amount of salt if you use salted butter or margarine.)

Flavorings

Flavorings such as vanilla and almond extracts are common ingredients in cookie recipes. Make sure to use pure (not artificial) extracts whenever possible. You can also flavor with whiskey, brandies, and rums.

Try using fresh citrus rinds. Grate only the outer colored layer of the fruit, leaving the white pith, which can be bitter.

Sugars

We are all trying to cut down on our sugar intake and this is the perfect place to start. You can control the amount and kind of sugar you put into your own recipes. We have sometimes used dried fruits such as raisins and dates to satisfy our craving for sweetness. This way we cannot be accused of consuming empty calories.

There are many sugars to choose from, aside from the usual white granulated kind. Each sweetener has its own flavor and texture. If you prefer a crunchy cookie, the drier, white granulated and raw sugars work well and can be interchanged in all the recipes. For a moister cookie, softer sugars such as confectioners' and soft brown sugar are well suited. Brown and raw sugars have a habit of going dry and hard, so store them in a tightly lidded jar with a piece of cut raw potato or a slice of lemon.

In the liquid sugar department you can choose from honey, molasses, and corn and maple syrup; all are natural sugars that add their own distinctive flavors to the finished product. You can mix and match these sugars to create something all your own. When measuring them, use a hot metal spoon to ensure accurate quantities.

Eggs

All the recipes in this book were tested using large eggs. Eggs whip to a greater volume when they are used at room temperature.

Nuts and Seeds

We prefer to buy whole, unskinned nuts, for both nutritional and aesthetic reasons. Toasting in an oven or toaster oven before chopping enhances their flavor. Store nuts in airtight containers.

Spices

Store them in a cool, dark place. Don't buy large quantities unless you plan to use them up quickly, as they lose their strength.

Chocolate

Chocolate chips may be made from squares by first freezing the chocolate for half an hour and then crushing it in a strong plastic bag with a rolling pin, as can be done with nuts.

When melting chocolate, make sure that the container in which you are melting it is absolutely dry. Melt it slowly over hot but not boiling water, as chocolate burns easily. Carob chips or squares can be substituted for chocolate wherever desired.

Decorations

There are all kinds of delightful and decadent things you can decorate cookies with. These are some of our suggestions:

- Sprinkle any one of the following on cookies while still warm:
  - confectioners' sugar, superfine sugar, or granulated sugar mixed with cinnamon
  - chocolate or candied sprinkles
  - chopped, crystallized, dried, or candied fruit

- seeds such as fennel, poppy, sesame, or pumpkin
- coconut flakes
- For a glossy varnish, beat an egg yolk, an egg white, or a whole egg lightly and brush on cookies before baking.
- Make a hollow in the top of the cookie with your thumb and drop jam into it.

Tools

Mixers

Our recipes have, in most cases, been made with both a food processor and an electric mixer. There is no difference in the final product. A food processor is no doubt quicker and more convenient, but it is by no means essential. Neither is an electric mixer for that matter.

Baking Sheets

Shiny aluminum cookie sheets without high sides (which deflect the heat) are ideal. They should be 2″ shorter and narrower than the oven so the heat can circulate, ensuring that the cookies brown evenly.

Two or more sheets allow you to operate like a production line, expertly filling one while the other bakes. Best results are obtained by baking one sheet at a time. It is not necessary to scrub your pans after each use. Just wipe them with a damp cloth so as not to scratch the surface or upset the buildup of oils.

Cookie Presses and Cutters

You can experiment with different utensils from your kitchen, such as forks, meat tenderizers, potato mashers, and thumbs, and all assortments of cutters and glasses. Create your own signature with a variety of shapes and imprints on your cookies!

SEED COOKIES

Plant a seed in your kitchen

CARAWAY

and watch its popularity grow like lichen

CARDAMOM

POPPY

SESAME

Caraway Seed Cookies

These cookies have such a distinct, delicious flavor that you'll get carried away, carrying them away.

½ cup	unsalted butter
½ cup	raw sugar
2	egg yolks
1 cup	all-purpose flour
1 cup	whole wheat flour
½ teaspoon	baking soda
½ cup	yogurt or sour cream
2 teaspoons	caraway seeds

1. Cream butter and sugar together until light and fluffy.
2. Beat in egg yolks and add half of each flour.
3. Add baking soda to sour cream, stir until double in volume, and add to dough with seeds.
4. Add remaining flour and mix until smooth.
5. Roll dough into a log shape 2" in diameter. Wrap and chill for 2 hours.
6. Cut into ¼" slices.
7. Sprinkle more seeds on top and press in with fingers.
8. Place on lightly greased baking sheet.
9. Bake at 350° for 15 minutes or until golden. Remove from oven and transfer to cooling rack.
   Yield: 40.

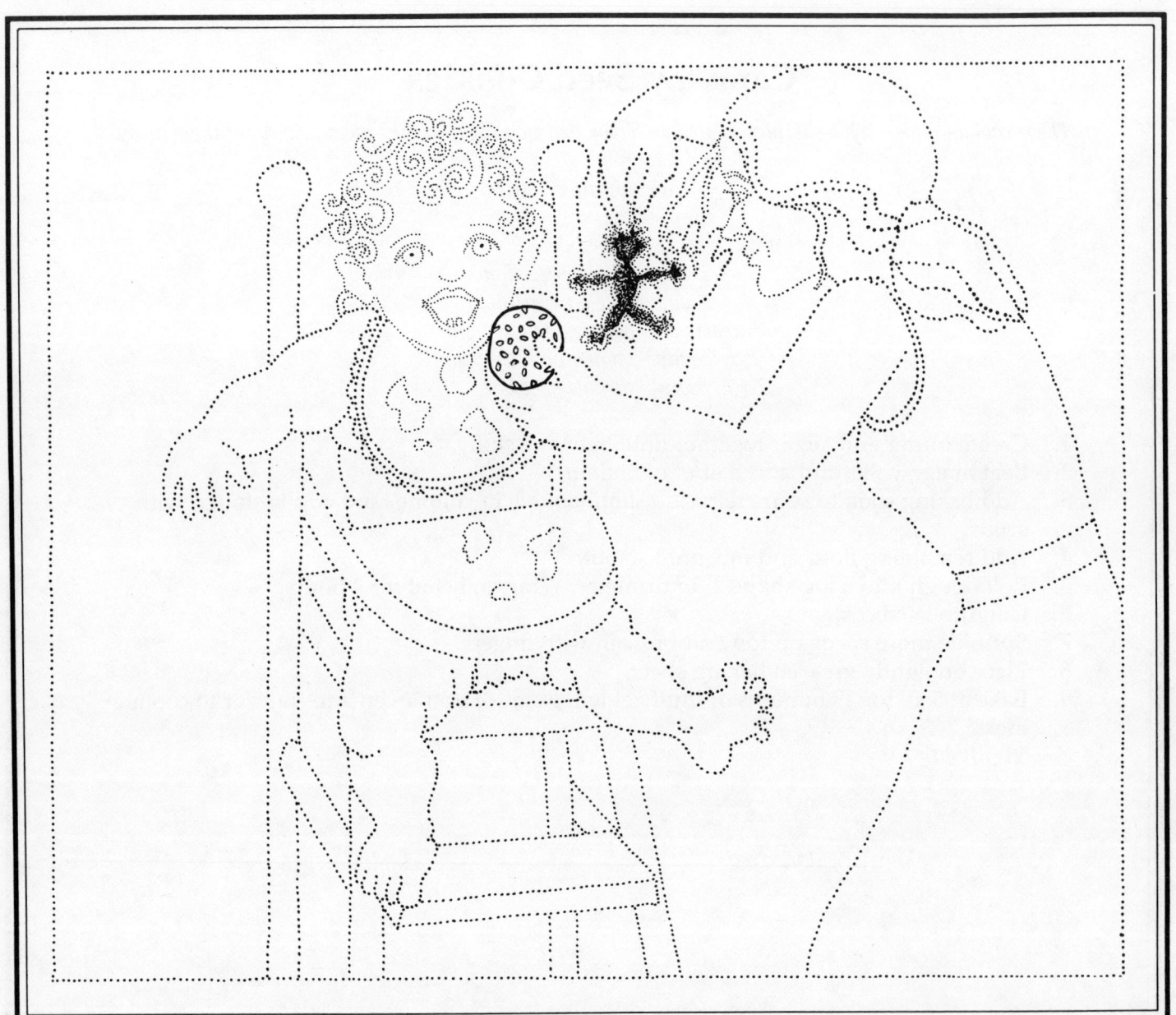

Open Sesames

Yum. . . ! is all we can say. If cookies could win a popularity contest, these would be our own choice for first place. They are much lighter and crispier than the typical sesame crunch, and brown sugar gives them a caramel taste.

¾ cup	sesame seeds
2 tablespoons	unsalted butter
1 cup	light brown sugar
2	egg yolks
2 teaspoons	vanilla extract
½ teaspoon	salt
5 tablespoons	all-purpose flour, sifted

1. Toast seeds in heavy frying pan over medium heat until golden. Set aside.
2. Melt butter. Remove from heat.
3. Stir in sugar, egg yolks, vanilla, and salt.
4. Add toasted seeds and then flour.
5. Place teaspoonfuls on greased baking sheet, leaving 2″ for spreading.
6. Bake at 350° for 12 minutes or until well browned.
7. Leave to set on baking sheet for no more than a minute. If cookies have set and are difficult to remove, return to oven for a couple of minutes and try again.
8. Carefully transfer to cooling rack, keeping cookies flat.
   Yield: 36.

Poppy Seed Cookies

Called Munn cookies in Jewish cuisine, these wafers are delicately flavored by the poppy seeds. They would be a lovely complement to an herbal tea as they are not too sweet. The dough must be frozen to facilitate wafer-thin slicing.

½ cup	unsalted butter
½ cup	corn oil
1½ cups	light brown sugar
1	egg
4 tablespoons	milk
¾ cup	poppy seeds
1 teaspoon	baking powder
1 cup	all-purpose flour
1½ cups	whole wheat flour
2½ cups	rolled oats
½ teaspoon	salt

1. Cream butter until light and fluffy, then add remaining ingredients.
2. Mix well. Dough should hold its shape but be slightly sticky.
3. Shape into 2 logs 2″ in diameter.
4. Wrap in waxed paper or plastic wrap and freeze overnight.
5. Cut while frozen into ⅛″ slices with very sharp knife.
6. Place on ungreased baking sheet. Reshape dough or press it thinner, if necessary, once on the sheet.
7. Bake at 350° for 10–12 minutes, or until lightly browned.
8. Lift carefully onto cooling rack. Cool flat.
   Yield: 7 dozen.

Cardamom Honey Pryanik

From Russia with love. These cookies are very unusual because of their distinct licorice flavor and their hard, crunchy texture.

¾ cup	unsalted butter
⅔ cup	soft brown sugar
2 tablespoons	honey
½ teaspoon	anise
¾ teaspoon	ground cardamom
2 teaspoons	cinnamon
¾ teaspoon	baking powder
¼ teaspoon	salt
½ cup	rye flour
1½ cups	whole wheat flour

1. Cream together butter, sugar, and honey.
2. Fold in all other ingredients; mix well.
3. Roll into walnut sized balls with wet hands.
4. Place on greased baking sheet.
5. Press down lightly with wet fork.
6. Bake at 350° for 12–15 minutes, or until set.
   Yield: 20.

NUT COOKIES

no need to panic
If you're not a mechanic,
No ifs, ands or buts
Just mix dough and nuts.

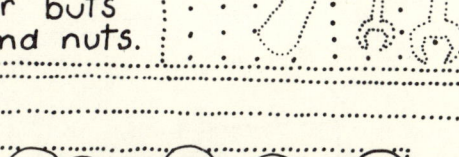

ALMOND CRESCENTS

CHINESE ALMONDS
SCREWS

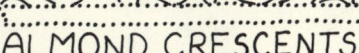

COCONUT CRUNCH

NAILS – 2"

HAZELNUTS

MANDELBREAD

NUTS

PEANUT BUTTER

BOLTS

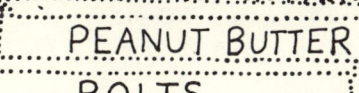

PECAN PEARLS

WALNUT RUGELACH

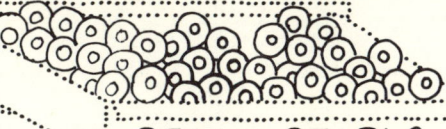

Almond Crescents

Whether these cookies are in the shapes of crescents, diamonds, squares, or kangaroos, they are delicious. The ingredients are few and are simple to prepare. The secret lies in the method of aerating the butter and sugar, ensuring a lighter-textured cookie.

1 cup	unsalted butter
½ cup	granulated sugar
1 cup	whole wheat flour
⅔ cup	all-purpose flour
⅔ cup	finely chopped almonds
¼ teaspoon	salt
	confectioners' sugar to dust

1. Cream butter and sugar until light and fluffy.
2. Fold in flours, almonds, and salt.
3. Shape into small crescents.
4. Place on ungreased baking sheet.
5. Bake at 350° for 10–15 minutes until lightly golden.
6. Remove from pan. Cool on wire rack.
7. When cool, dust with confectioners' sugar.
   Yield: 35.

Chinese Almond Cookies

One of the fondest memories of Diane's childhood in Montreal is the weekly ritual of dining with the family in the local Chinese restaurant. Their Chinese almond cookie was the perfect conclusion to that feast. Here is the reincarnation of that mystical cookie.

¼ cup	lard
¼ cup	unsalted butter
1 cup	granulated sugar
1 teaspoon	baking soda
2 teaspoons	water
1	egg
1teaspoon	almond extract
½ cup	rice flour
1½ cups	cake flour
15	whole almonds

1. Cream together lard, butter, and sugar until light and fluffy.
2. Dissolve soda in water; add to creamed mixture.
3. Beat in egg and almond extract.
4. Fold in the sifted flours, adding a little extra flour if mixture seems too soft.
5. With wet palms, roll into 30 balls.
6. Place on greased baking sheet, allowing 3″ for spreading.
7. Press halved almond into each ball.
8. Bake at 350° for 12–15 minutes or until edges begin to brown.
9. Remove from pans; cool on rack.
   Yield: 30.

Coconut Crunch

We will just make it short and sweet. They are crunchy, munchy, and irresistible to eat.

⅔ cup	unsalted butter
½ cup	raw sugar
1½ cups	whole wheat flour
1⅓ cups	shredded coconut
¼ teaspoon	salt
	milk for brushing
⅓ cup	coconut for topping

1. Mix butter, sugar, flour, coconut, and salt until mixture resembles fine breadcrumbs.
2. Knead gently for a few minutes.
3. Wrap and chill for 1 hour.
4. Roll out to ¼" thick, and cut into round shapes with a glass or a cookie cutter.
5. Place on greased baking sheet.
6. Brush with a little milk and sprinkle with coconut.
7. Bake at 350° for 12–15 minutes or until golden.
8. Remove from pan and cool on wire rack.
   Yield: 36.

Hazelnut Cookies

The hazelnuts and raw sugar give this cookie a crispy texture and delicious flavor. There are many interpretations of this kind of cookie but we find this the most successful. Thank you, Bonnie Stern!

1 cup	unsalted butter
1 cup	raw sugar
1	egg yolk
1 teaspoon	vanilla extract
1¼ cups	finely chopped hazelnuts
1 cup	whole wheat flour
1 cup	all-purpose flour

1. Cream butter and sugar until light and fluffy.
2. Mix in egg yolk and vanilla extract.
3. Add 1 cup chopped hazelnuts and whole wheat and all-purpose flours.
4. Form dough into 1″ balls and arrange on greased baking sheet.
5. Flatten balls with wet fork in crisscross pattern.
6. Sprinkle with remainder of nuts.
7. Bake at 350° for 15–20 minutes or until lightly brown and set.
8. Remove from oven and transfer to cooling rack.
   Yield: 5 dozen.

Mandelbread

The recipe for these traditional Jewish cookies was sifted down through four generations until it has finally been recorded for posterity in this book. They are very simple to make. The secret to their crispness is returning them to a warm oven for half an hour after they have been baked.

1 cup	corn oil
1 cup	raw sugar
3	eggs
½ teaspoon	salt
1 teaspoon	vanilla extract
1 teaspoon	almond extract
2 teaspoons	baking powder
¼ teaspoon	nutmeg
¼ teaspoon	cinnamon
1½ cups	whole wheat flour
1 cup	all-purpose flour
1 cup	coarsely chopped walnuts or almonds
¼ cup	granulated sugar mixed with 1 tablespoon cinnamon

1. Mix together oil, sugar, eggs, salt, vanilla, and almond extract.
2. Mix together the baking powder, spices, flours, and nuts. Fold in until well mixed. (This mixture will be quite soft and sticky, but not runny. If it is runny, add a little more flour.)
3. Form into 3 log shapes on greased baking sheet.
4. Sprinkle with some of the sugar-cinnamon mixture.
5. Bake at 350° for 40 minutes.
6. Cut into ¾" slices, and spread apart leaving slices upright.
7. Return to warm oven (225°) for 30 minutes.
   Yield: 45.

Peanut Butter Cookies

Peanut butter is very versatile and is ideally suited as the main ingredient for a children's snack. We prefer to use a crunchy peanut butter and to add extra chopped nuts to give a crisp, nutty texture. We recommend a peanut butter with as few additives as possible to ensure that the flavor of this recipe remains unaltered.

½ cup	unsalted butter
½ cup	peanut butter
½ cup	soft brown sugar
½ cup	granulated sugar
1	egg
½ teaspoon	vanilla extract
1 tablespoon	grated orange rind
1½ cups	whole wheat flour
¼ teaspoon	salt
½ cup	chopped peanuts
½ teaspoon	baking soda

1. Cream butter, peanut butter, and sugars together until light and fluffy.
2. Add egg, vanilla, and orange rind. Mix well.
3. Combine flour, salt, peanuts, and soda, and stir into mixture until well blended.
4. Drop heaping teaspoonfuls onto a greased baking sheet, allowing 2″ for spreading.
5. Bake at 350° for 10–12 minutes or until lightly browned and set.
6. Remove from oven and transfer to cooling rack.
   Yield: 40.

Pecan Pearls

The ground pecans make this cookie exotically decadent and rich. They crumble easily because they are so light!

1 cup	unsalted butter
2 teaspoons	vanilla extract
4 tablespoons	raw sugar
2 cups	cake flour
1 cup	finely ground pecans
	confectioners' sugar

1. Cream butter, vanilla, and sugar until creamy and light.
2. Fold in flour and nuts until well mixed.
3. Roll tablespoonfuls of dough into balls and place on ungreased baking sheet.
4. Press a hollow into the center of each ball with your thumb.
5. Bake at 300° for about 30 minutes.
6. Sprinkle with sifted confectioners' sugar while still warm.
   Yield: 20.

For a variation substitute walnuts for the pecans.

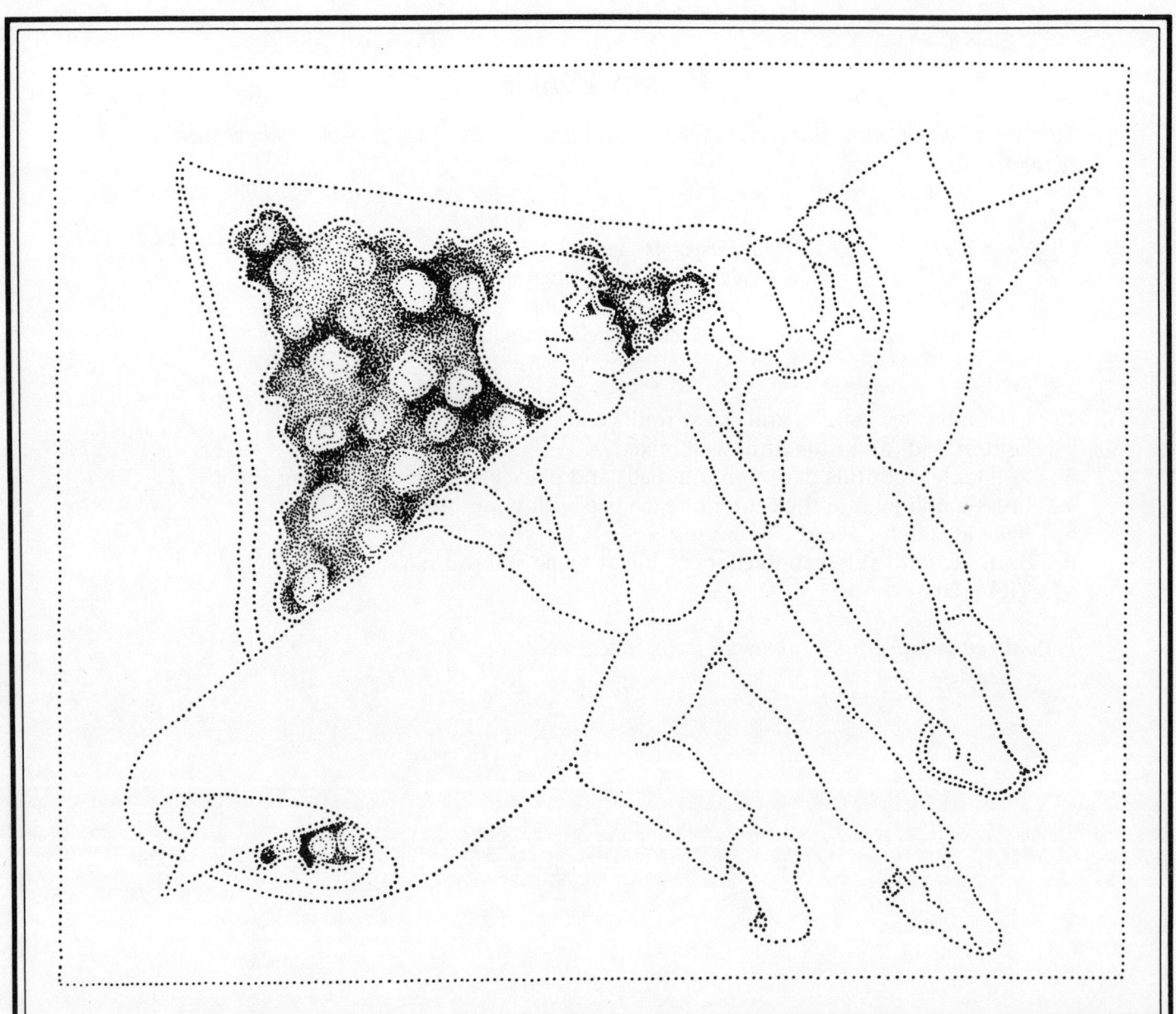

Walnut Rugelach

The cream cheese pastry is sweetened by the filling of jam, sugar, and cinnamon. The nuts give them an extra bite. These biscuits are rich and extravagant and are for people who feel likewise. Those who need to be creative can experiment endlessly with different combinations of fillings.

Dough
1 cup	unsalted butter
1 cup	cream cheese
2 cups	all-purpose flour

Filling
½ cup	strawberry jam
2 cups	chopped walnuts
6 tablespoons	granulated sugar mixed with
	2 tablespoons cinnamon

1. Cream butter and cheese together until well blended.
2. Add flour and mix with cool hands (if dough is sticky add a little more flour).
3. Divide dough into three pieces and chill for 30 minutes.
4. Roll each piece into a circle ⅛" thick.
5. Spread thinly with jam. Sprinkle with walnuts; then cover liberally with sugar mixture.
6. Cut each circle into 16 triangles and roll each one up, wide side first.
7. Place on greased baking sheet; bake at 350° for 20 minutes.
8. Remove from oven and transfer to cooling rack.
   Yield: 48.

WHOLE WHEAT COOKIES

WHOLE WHEAT
WHOLE SOME

GRANOLA BARS

GERARD'S
BUCKWHEAT
INVENTIONS

HEALTHY
WEALTHY
COOKIES

MOLASSES
FLAPJACKS

WHOLE TREATS
WHOLE FUN

MUESLI

SCOTTISH
OATCAKES

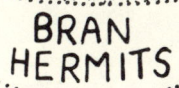

BRAN
HERMITS

RIA'S
ZIG-ZOGS

Gerard's Buckwheat Inventions

A young, creative chef in Penrith, England, shared his inventions with us. This crumbly, wholesome cookie is the only one in this book that relies solely on natural sweetness for its flavoring.

⅔ cup	lightly toasted buckwheat
1¼ cups	whole wheat flour
1 cup	rolled oats
⅔ cup	lightly toasted cashews, chopped
⅔ cup	currants
2 tablespoons	rice flour
2 teaspoons	cinnamon
1 teaspoon	ground ginger
½ teaspoon	salt
1	egg
3 tablespoons	honey
4–5 tablespoons	vegetable oil

1. Mix together all dry ingredients.
2. Add beaten egg, honey, and oil and mix until mixture holds together.
3. Press into oiled 8″ × 12″ jelly roll pan.
4. Bake at 325° for 30 minutes or until lightly brown and set.
5. Cut hot and leave in pan to cool.
   Yield: 24.

Healthy Wealthy Cookies

This is our most extravagant cookie! The nutritious, delicious result is well worth the investment.

1 cup	unsalted butter
½ cup	peanut butter
1½ cups	raw sugar
2	eggs
1 cup	whole wheat flour
1 cup	rolled oats
½ cup	wheat germ
1 teaspoon	baking powder
¾ teaspoon	salt
1 tablespoon	cinnamon
½ teaspoon	each, of ground ginger and nutmeg
1 cup	each of coarsely chopped walnuts, pecans, and peanuts
1½ cups	raisins
½ cup	each, of sunflower seeds, pine nuts, and sesame seeds

1. Cream together butter, peanut butter and sugar.
2. Beat in eggs.
3. In large bowl, combine all other dry ingredients.
4. Add butter mixture to dry ingredients. Mix well with hands.
5. Roll into 1" balls with wet hands and then flatten with the bottom of a glass.
6. Bake at 350° for 18–20 minutes or until lightly browned.
7. Carefully remove cookies to wire rack to cool.
   Yield: 40 cookies.

Molasses Flapjacks

Our good friends Geoff and Dorothy Snell serve this version of the traditional flapjack in their whole-food cafe at Wetheriggs Pottery in Penrith, England. The molasses accounts for its dark, chewy wholesomeness.

½ cup	unsalted butter
⅓ cup	soft brown sugar
⅓ cup	molasses
⅓ cup	coarsely chopped mixed dried fruit
3–3½ cups	rolled oats

1. Melt butter, sugar, and molasses over low heat.
2. Stir in fruit and as many oats as can be absorbed.
3. Roll dough into 1" balls and flatten with the bottom of a glass or a spatula.
4. Bake at 350° for 15–20 minutes or until set.
5. Transfer to cooling rack.
   Yield: 34.

Muesli Pieces

These salubrious biscuits are ideal for the on-the-go health freak as they provide a nutritious in-between-meal snack. It's one cookie we encourage our own children to eat and is simple enough for them to make. You'll find in the baking process that the pieces are very crumbly until they cool.

1 cup	unsalted butter
¾ cup	raw sugar
1½ tablespoons	honey
2 cups	muesli
2 cups	whole wheat flour
½ cup	sunflower seeds
½ cup	sesame seeds

1. In large saucepan melt butter, sugar, and honey.
2. Add all other ingredients; mix well.
3. Press into greased 8″ × 12″ jelly roll pan.
4. Bake at 325° for 30 minutes.
5. Cut into squares while still warm.
6. Carefully transfer to wire rack to cool.
   Yield: 24.

Scottish Oatcakes

These savory cookies are more like a cracker and are a great complement for cheese. People without a sweet tooth may find themselves nibbling these around the clock.

6 tablespoons	unsalted butter
6 tablespoons	lard
½ cup	granulated sugar
2 cups	whole wheat flour
2½ cups	rolled oats
½ teaspoon	salt
½ teaspoon	baking soda
3–4 tablespoons	milk

1. Place all ingredients except milk in large bowl.
2. Mix with hands or mixer/processor until it has the consistency of breadcrumbs.
3. Add enough milk to bind mixture.
4. Chill for 30 minutes.
5. Roll out to ¼″ thick and cut into rounds with a glass or cutters.
6. Place on ungreased baking sheet. Bake at 400° for 10 minutes.
7. Carefully transfer to wire rack to cool.
   Yield: 30.

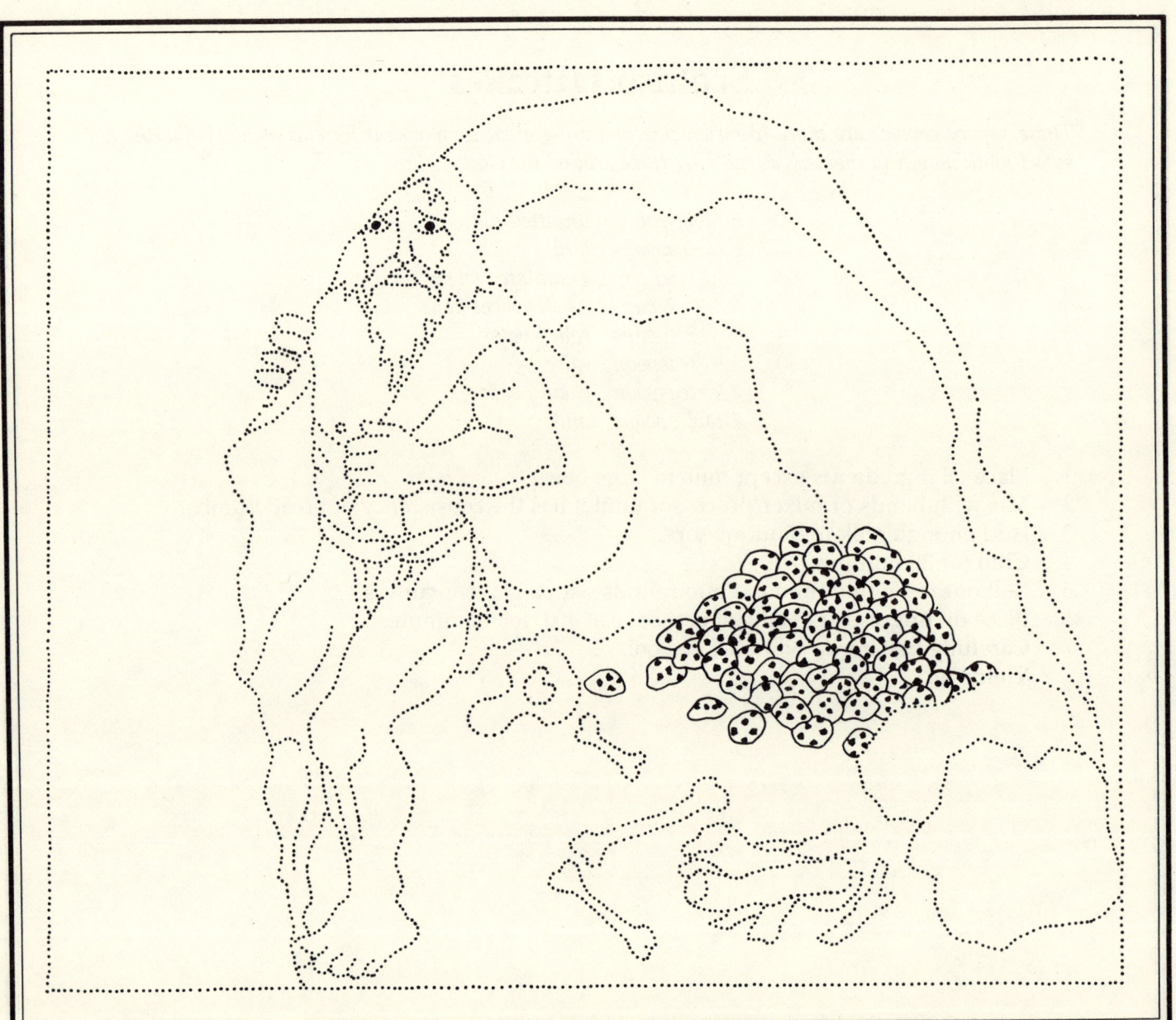

Bran Hermits

This is a most palatable way of increasing fiber in your daily diet. We have chosen All-Bran cereal instead of plain bran, as it produces a moister cookie with the same results.

½ cup	unsalted butter
⅔ cup	soft brown sugar
1	egg, beaten
1 teaspoon	vanilla extract
1 cup	whole wheat flour
1 cup	All-Bran cereal
½ cup	chopped mixed nuts
½ cup	chopped dates
2 teaspoons	cinnamon
1 teaspoon	baking soda
1 teaspoon	baking powder
¼ teaspoon	salt

1. Cream together butter and sugar.
2. Add egg and vanilla extract.
3. Stir other ingredients together; add to creamed mixture and mix well.
4. Drop by tablespoonfuls onto greased baking tray.
5. Bake at 350° for 12–15 minutes, or until edges are lightly browned.
6. Cool on wire rack.
   Yield: 25.

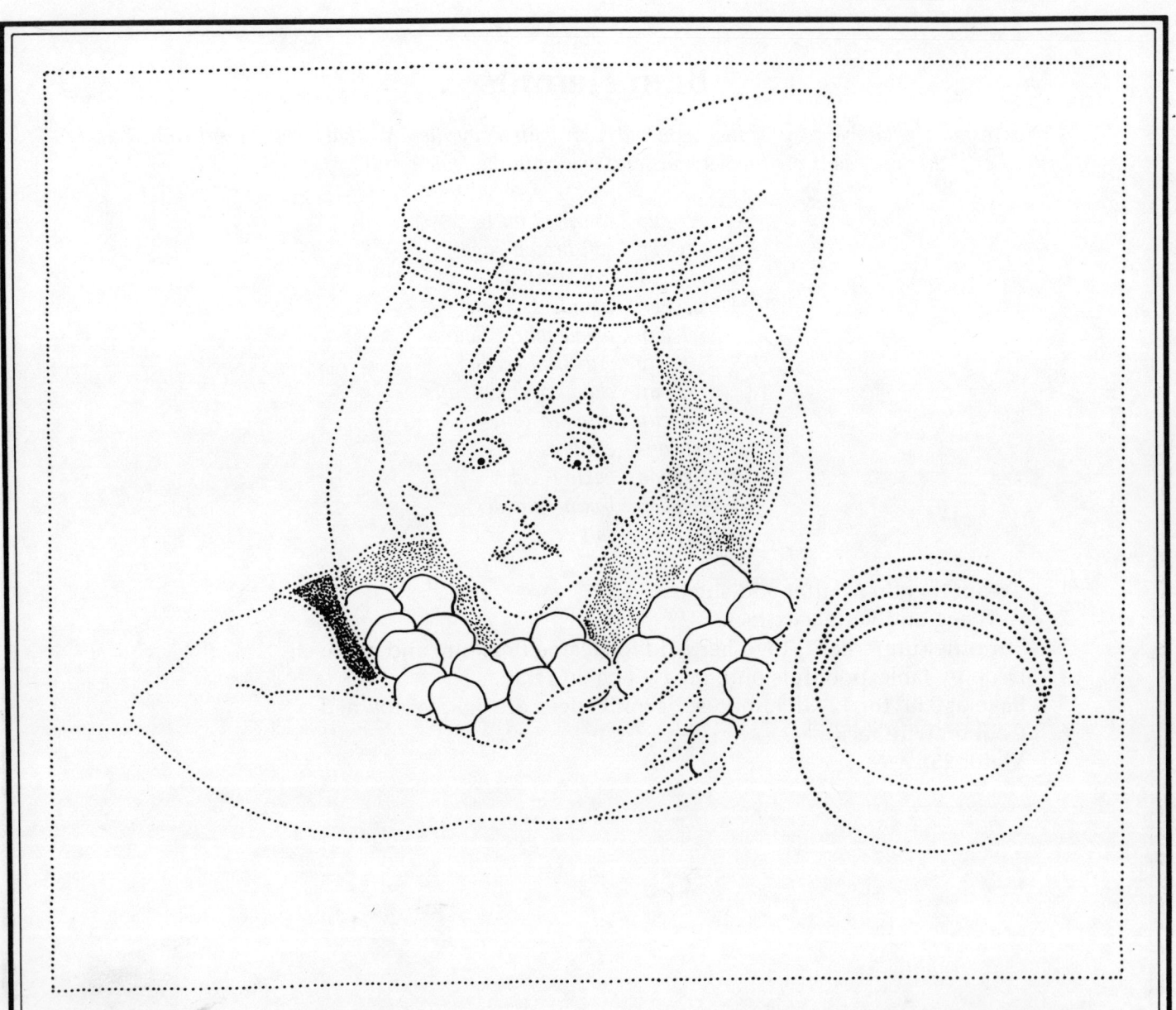

Ria's Zig-Zogs

This chunky cookie is one you should keep within your children's reach. It is so simple and cheap to make that we often double the quantities.

¾ cup	butter or margarine
2 tablespoons	corn syrup or honey
1½ cups	whole wheat flour
2 cups	rolled oats
1 scant cup	raw sugar
1 teaspoon	baking soda
¼ teaspoon	salt

1. In large pan melt butter with syrup.
2. Remove from heat and add all dry ingredients; mix well.
3. Form heaping teaspoonfuls of mixture into balls.
4. Place on greased baking sheet, allowing 2" for spreading.
5. Bake at 350° for 10–15 minutes or until golden. Transfer to cooling rack.
   Yield: 20.

Granola Bars

These bars will easily be considered as good as gold in your household. There is room for experiment-ing—you can use our granola recipe (on page 68) or your own, substituting nuts or spices to your own taste. The result is inevitably a memorable one when the bars are coated with the honey glaze.

4 cups	granola mix
1 cup	whole wheat flour
½ teaspoon	baking soda
1 teaspoon	cinnamon
½ teaspoon	allspice
¾ cup	unsalted butter
2	eggs, beaten
1 teaspoon	vanilla
¼ cup	honey (to glaze)

1. In large bowl combine granola, flour, soda, and spices.
2. Melt butter; remove from heat.
3. Add eggs and vanilla to melted butter, stirring constantly.
4. Pour butter mixture over dry ingredients and mix well with wooden spoon.
5. Turn into 15″ × 10″ × 1″ greased jelly roll pan and press down lightly with a spoon.
6. Bake at 375° for 15–20 minutes until firm and lightly browned.
7. Warm honey and brush it over top.
8. Cut while warm; leave to cool in tray.
    Yield: 36.

Granola Mix

6 cups	rolled oats
1 cup	wheat germ
1 cup	sunflower seeds
½ cup	sesame seeds
½ cup	shredded coconut
¼ teaspoon	salt
1 teaspoon	cinnamon
½ teaspoon	nutmeg
1 cup	chopped almonds or peanuts
⅔ cup	vegetable oil
⅔ cup	honey
1 cup	raisins

1. Combine the first nine ingredients in large bowl.
2. Heat together oil and honey until warm and blended.
3. Pour warm mixture over dry ingredients; stir until evenly mixed.
4. Spread mixture evenly in two large jelly roll pans.
5. Bake at 225° for 30 minutes, stirring frequently until evenly browned.
6. Add raisins during last 10 minutes.
7. Cool and store in airtight container.
   Yield: 11 cups.

SHORTBREADS

TAKE A SHORTCUT

COFFEE-TOFFEE

CASHEW

COCONUT

MAKE SHORTBREADS

PEPPERMINT

WHOLE WHEAT

THEY'RE SURE TO BE SHORTLIVED

Cashew Shortbread

The "short" in shortbread refers to the texture of the cookie. It is dense and crispy. The addition of nuts enhances this quality.

½ cup	unsalted butter
⅓ cup	raw sugar
1 cup	whole wheat flour
½ cup	rice flour
	pinch of salt
½ cup	finely chopped cashews, lightly toasted
	granulated sugar

1. Mix together butter, raw sugar, flour, rice flour, and salt until it has the consistency of breadcrumbs.
2. Add cashews and knead gently until mixture holds together.
3. Roll into 1" balls; place on ungreased baking sheet.
4. Press with fork or cookie press.
5. Bake at 350° for 10–12 minutes until just golden.
6. Sprinkle with granulated sugar while warm.
   Yield: 20.

For a variation, substitute finely chopped almonds for the cashews.

Coconut Puffs

These shortbread cookies are a hedonist's delight! The refined ingredients of cake flour and confectioners' sugar make them melt in your mouth. Be sure to watch them closely in the oven so that the finished result is as white as driven snow.

1 cup	unsalted butter
½ cup	confectioners' sugar
½ cup	desiccated coconut
2 cups	sifted cake flour

1. Cream butter and sugar for about 5 minutes until very light and fluffy.
2. Add coconut and mix carefully.
3. Add sifted flour until just blended.
4. Carefully roll into 1″ balls with cool damp hands.
5. Place on ungreased baking sheet; press lightly with cookie press.
6. Bake at 350° for 10–15 minutes or until set.
   Yield: 20.

Instructions for using a shortbread mold

1. Grease and flour mold.
2. Pat a piece of dough into mold to ½″ thickness.
3. Carefully invert onto ungreased baking sheet.
4. Bake at 325° for approximately 20 minutes. (Baking time varies with size of mold.)

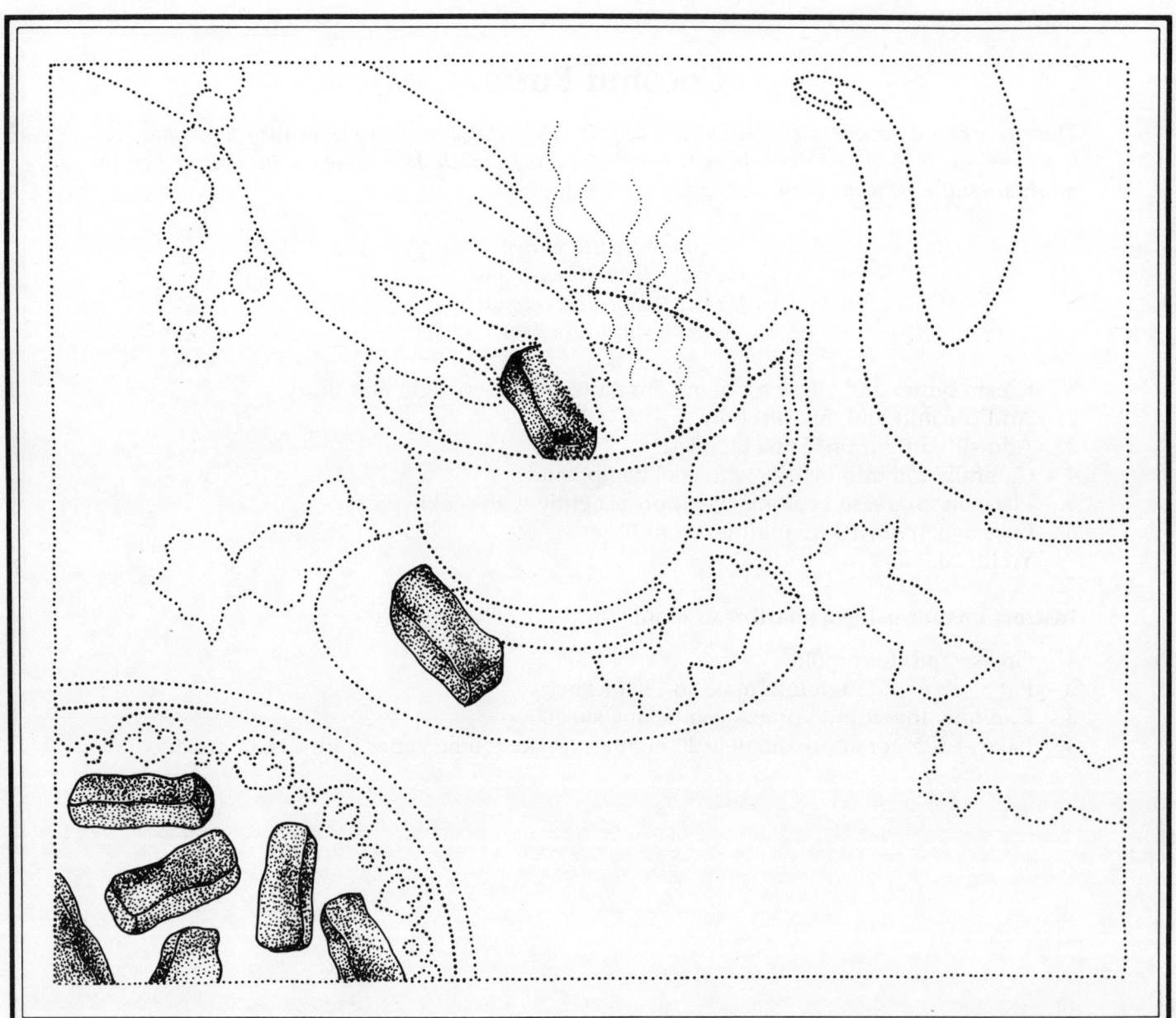

Coffee-Toffee Shortbread

This is softer than usual shortbread, and is covered with chocolate and chopped nuts.

1 cup	unsalted butter
1⅓ cups	soft brown sugar
1	egg yolk
1 teaspoon	vanilla extract
1½ teaspoons	coffee extract or very strong coffee
1½ cups	all-purpose flour
1½ cups	whole wheat flour
6 ounces	semisweet chocolate chips
1 cup	chopped walnuts or hazelnuts

1. Cream butter and sugar until light and fluffy.
2. Add egg yolk and extracts.
3. Stir in flours until well mixed.
4. Pat dough into greased 8″ × 12″ × 1″ baking pan.
5. Bake at 350° for 20 minutes.
6. Remove from oven. Sprinkle chocolate on hot biscuit and, when melted, spread with knife.
7. Sprinkle with chopped nuts.
8. Cut while warm, leave to cool in pan.
   Yield: 24.

Chocolate Peppermint Shortbread

The combination of shortbread, chocolate, and peppermint is rich, refreshing, and festive just like Christmas, when they are traditionally baked. Even though these cookies are simple to make, we exercise restraint and only prepare them on special occasions or for special people.

Shortbread

⅔ cup	unsalted butter
2¼ cups	whole wheat flour
½ cup	soft brown sugar
2 tablespoons	cocoa powder
¼ teaspoon	salt

Peppermint icing

2 teaspoons	peppermint extract
3-4 tablespoons	water
2¼ cups	sifted confectioners' sugar
6 ounces (squares)	semisweet chocolate

1. Mix together all ingredients for shortbread.
2. Knead gently. Press into greased 8″ × 12″ pan.
3. Bake at 325° for 45–60 minutes or until edges are lightly browned.
4. Stir peppermint extract into water and gradually mix with confectioners' sugar until thick and pastelike.
5. Spread icing on warm shortbread. Leave to set slightly, about 10 minutes.
6. Melt chocolate over hot water and then spread over icing.
7. Carefully cut with hot knife when chocolate is semiset. Leave to cool in pan.
   Yield: 24 bars.

Whole Wheat Shortbread

We first tasted this wholesome shortbread in Kendal, England, in a health food cafe, and then experimented with this recipe at home. The raw sugar gives the cookie its crisp crunchiness. The secret lies in baking the shortbread slowly.

½ cup	unsalted butter
1¼ cups	whole wheat flour
2 tablespoons	rice flour
⅓ cup	raw sugar
¼ teaspoon	salt
	granulated sugar

1. Place all ingredients except granulated sugar in bowl.
2. Mix to a breadcrumblike consistency.
3. Knead lightly until mixture holds together.
4. Wrap and chill dough for half an hour in refrigerator.
5. Roll out on floured board to ¼" thick. Cut with cookie cutter.
6. Place on ungreased baking sheet.
7. Bake at 300° for 25 minutes or until just golden.
8. Sprinkle with granulated sugar while warm.
   Yield: 20.

Ginger Shortbread

Add 2 teaspoons ground ginger to mixture at stage 1.
If using shortbread molds for either of the above, follow instructions as for coconut puffs.

Maple Shortbread

1. Boil 1 cup maple syrup to 250°.
2. Pour into greased baking pan, leave to cool, and then freeze.
3. Crush maple sugar while frozen. Use as above in place of raw sugar, but double the quantity.

CHOCOLATE COOKIES

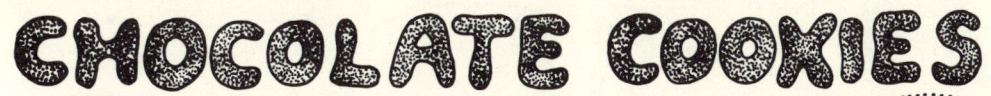

INSTEAD OF EATING A CHOCOLATE BAR:
CURL IT, WHIRL IT, CHIP IT, DIP IT,
WHIP IT, SIP IT, ICE IT, SLICE IT,
GRATE IT AND MATE IT IN THE FOLLOWING
COOKIE CORNUCOPIAS

☆ CHOCOLATE CHIP I ☆ CHOCOLATE CHIP II ☆ DIANE'S DREAM'S

HELENE'S
☆ FLORENTINE'S ☆   CHOCOLATE
RICE DATE CRISPIES   ☆   CHOCOLATE
MULATTOES

Chocolate Chip Cookies

This all-time favorite speaks for itself!

½ cup	unsalted butter
½ cup	granulated sugar
½ cup	soft brown sugar
½ teaspoon	vanilla extract
1	egg
1¼ cups	sifted cake flour
¼ teaspoon	salt
1 cup	chocolate chips

1. Cream together butter, sugars, and vanilla.
2. Beat in egg.
3. Fold in flour, salt, and chocolate chips.
4. Drop in heaping teaspoonfuls onto greased baking sheet, allowing 2" for spreading.
5. Bake at 350° for 12–15 minutes, or until edges are lightly browned.
6. Remove from pan; cool on wire rack.
   Yield: 38.

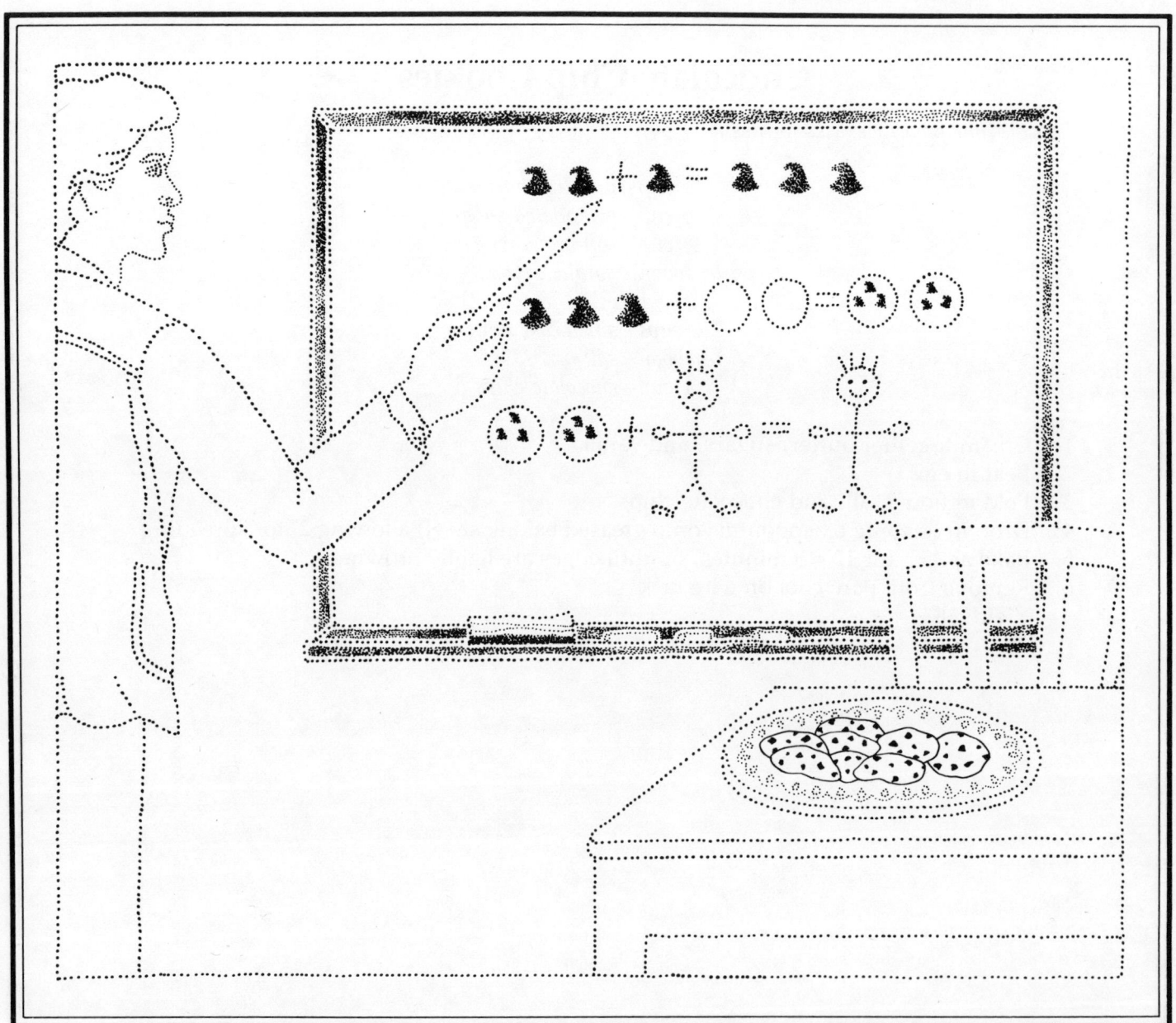

Chocolate Chip Plus

(whole wheat and almond)

This interpretation of the inimitable chocolate chip cookie doesn't need an interpreter. It is packed full of not only chocolate chips, but the protein value of nuts and whole wheat and soy flours.

1 cup	unsalted butter
1 cup	raw sugar
1 teaspoon	vanilla extract
1 teaspoon	almond extract
¼ teaspoon	salt
2	eggs
1 cup	whole wheat flour
½ cup	soy flour
½ cup	all-purpose flour
2 cups	chocolate chips
1 cup	toasted almonds, chopped

1. Beat together butter, sugar, vanilla extract, almond extract, and salt until creamy.
2. Beat in eggs one at a time.
3. Sift all flours together (tipping in any bran left in the sieve) and add to butter mixture.
4. Add chocolate chips and almonds and stir well to combine.
5. Drop by heaping teaspoonfuls onto greased baking sheet, allowing 2″ for spreading.
6. Bake at 350° for 9–12 minutes or until edges are lightly browned.
7. Lift carefully onto rack to cool.
   Yield: 30.

Chocolate Mulattoes

Life can never be black and white again once you have experienced these cookies. Try them—they are bound to resolve any dispute.

10 ounces (squares)	semisweet chocolate
4 tablespoons	unsalted butter
½ cup	whole wheat flour
½ teaspoon	baking powder
¼ teaspoon	salt
2	eggs
¾ cup	soft brown sugar
4 teaspoons	coffee extract or very strong coffee
1 teaspoon	vanilla extract
1½ cups	chocolate chips
2½ cups	chopped walnuts

1. Melt chocolate squares and butter in bowl over pan of hot water; set aside to cool.
2. Mix together flour, baking powder, and salt; set aside.
3. Beat together eggs, sugar, coffee, and vanilla extracts for 2 minutes.
4. Add cooled chocolate mixture to dry ingredients. Mix well.
5. Stir in chocolate chips and chopped walnuts.
6. Drop in heaping teaspoonfuls onto greased baking sheet, allowing 2″ for spreading.
7. Bake at 350° for 15–20 minutes or until set and firm.
8. Remove from pan and cool flat on wire rack.
   Yield: 40-45.

Chocolate Rice Date Crispies

You'll want a date with a nutritious date cookie every day of the year. They are sweet, chewy, and simple to make. No baking required.

½ cup	unsalted butter
1 cup	chopped dates
⅔ cup	raw sugar
3 cups	Rice Krispies
4 ounces (squares)	semisweet chocolate

1. Cook together butter, dates, and sugar, stirring constantly over low heat for 3–5 minutes until fudgelike.
2. Remove from heat and stir in Rice Krispies until well blended.
3. Press into 8″ × 12″ × 1″ jelly roll pan.
4. Melt chocolate over hot water.
5. Spread it over mixture.
6. Chill in refrigerator for 2 hours.
7. Cut into squares when cold.
   Yield: 24.

Diane's Dreams

The basic ingredients of walnuts, chocolate, and cloves create a unique flavor. Combined with a meringuelike texture, they are everybody's dreams, not only Diane's.

2 tablespoons	unsalted butter
1¾ cups	raw sugar
2	eggs
1 teaspoon	ground cloves
1 teaspoon	cinnamon
¼ cup	bran
2 tablespoons	whole wheat flour
2 cups	chopped walnuts
3 ounces (squares)	coarsely chopped semisweet chocolate

1. Beat together butter, sugar, eggs, and spices until thick and creamy.
2. Combine bran, flour, chopped walnuts, and chopped chocolate.
3. Add dry mixture to butter mixture until just blended.
4. Place 1" balls onto greased baking sheet.
5. Bake at 350° for 12–15 minutes or until set.
6. Cool on wire rack.
   Yield: 30.

Helene's Florentines

Helene deserves all the credit for the best version of this decadent delicacy and we are grateful that she has permitted us to share her secret with you.

6 tablespoons	unsalted butter
⅔ cup	raw sugar
½ cup	roughly chopped almonds
½ cup	roughly chopped hazelnuts
½ cup	roughly chopped walnuts
2 tablespoons	grated orange rind
1 tablespoon	orange juice
⅓ cup	sultanas
⅓ cup	chopped glacé cherries
1	egg
2 tablespoons	whole wheat flour
5–6 ounces (squares)	semisweet chocolate, melted

1. Melt butter and sugar over low heat.
2. Stir in remaining ingredients except chocolate.
3. Line two baking sheets with baking parchment.
4. Place heaping tablespoonfuls onto paper allowing 3″ for spreading.
5. Bake at 350° for 15 minutes, or until edges become brown.
6. Allow to cool slightly before carefully removing to wire rack.
7. When cold, spread bottoms of florentines with melted chocolate.
   Yield: 14.

SPICE COOKIES

HERE'S SOME ADVICE FOR THE TAKING:
SPICE UP YOUR LIFE WITH YOUR BAKING.

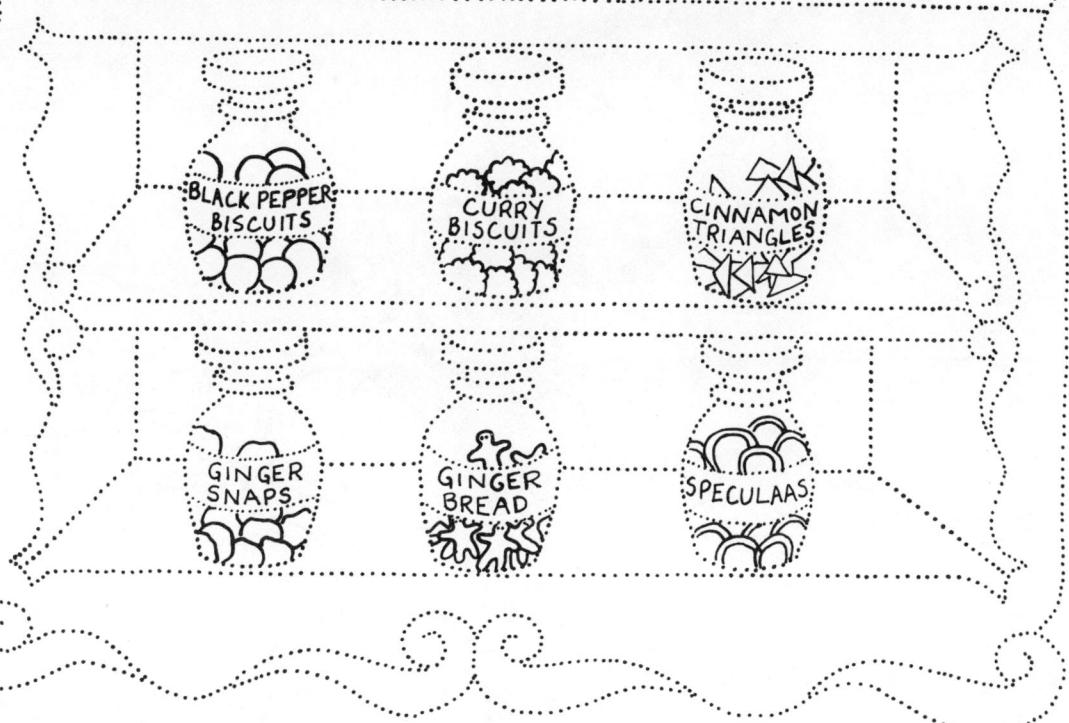

Black Pepper Biscuits

The subtle hotness of the black pepper becomes more pronounced and more addictive with each bite. We especially enjoy these cookies with a cup of coffee.

1 cup	unsalted butter
1½ cups	raw sugar
¾ teaspoon	freshly ground black pepper
pinch	cayenne pepper
½ teaspoon	ground cloves
1 tablespoon	cinnamon
1 tablespoon	ground ginger
1	egg
2 cups	whole wheat flour
1 cup	all-purpose flour
2 teaspoons	baking powder

1. Cream butter and sugar with all spices.
2. Beat in egg.
3. Mix in flours and baking powder.
4. Turn out onto floured surface and knead lightly.
5. Roll out to ¼″ thick and cut with cookie cutter.
6. Bake at 400° for 10–12 minutes or until lightly brown.
7. Cool on wire rack.
   Yield: 50.

Curry Biscuits

The curry in this esoteric cookie guarantees it will be a hot property in anyone's kitchen. There is a symbiotic relationship between these cookies and blue Stilton cheese.

1½ cups	whole wheat flour
½ cup	rolled oats
4 teaspoons	granulated sugar
1 teaspoon	baking powder
pinch	salt
½ teaspoon	curry powder
¼ cup	lard
¼ cup	unsalted butter
2 tablespoons	milk

1. Place dry ingredients in large bowl.
2. Add lard and butter. Mix to a breadcrumblike consistency.
3. Add enough milk to bind dough.
4. Knead for a few minutes.
5. Roll out to ¼" thick on floured surface.
6. Cut with a glass or a cookie cutter.
7. Place on ungreased baking sheet.
8. Bake at 350° for 15 minutes.
   Yield: 25.

Cinnamon Triangles

Cookie dough plus cinnamon plus almonds equals a perfectly balanced result. The whole is even greater than the sum of its parts!

2 cups	whole wheat flour
½ cup	rice flour
	pinch of salt
1 cup	soft brown sugar
1 cup	unsalted butter
1½ tablespoons	cinnamon
1	egg, separated
½ cup	sliced almonds

1. Place flours, salt, sugar, butter, cinnamon, and egg yolk in bowl. Mix until blended.
2. Turn out onto lightly floured board and knead lightly.
3. Press into greased 8″ × 12″ × 1″ jelly roll pan.
4. Brush with egg white. Sprinkle sliced almonds onto dough.
5. Bake at 325° for 20–30 minutes or until edges are lightly browned.
6. Cut while warm, first into squares and then across each square diagonally.
7. Carefully lift onto wire rack to cool.
   Yield: 30.

Ginger Snaps

This fail-safe recipe produces an irresistible hard and crunchy cookie that is snapped up as soon as it is baked.

1 cup	margarine
4 tablespoons	pure maple syrup
3½ cups	cake flour
4 teaspoons	ground ginger
⅔ cup	rolled oats
1⅓ cups	granulated sugar
1 teaspoon	baking soda
2 tablespoons	cold water

1. Melt margarine and syrup over low heat.
2. In large bowl, sift flour with ginger.
3. Add oats and sugar; stir.
4. Pour margarine over dry ingredients.
5. Dissolve soda in water and add to mixture. Mix well with wooden spoon.
6. Roll into 1" balls with wet hands. Press with glass or cookie press.
7. Place on greased baking sheet, leaving 3" for spreading.
8. Bake at 300° for 20–25 minutes or until browned and crispy.
9. Cool slightly, then remove from pan.

Yield: 35-40.

Gingerbread Men

This version of gingerbread will be a favorite with young and old. It is a very hardy dough that can be handled easily, and when baked turns into that traditional cookie we all love.

1¼ cups	all-purpose flour
⅔ cup	soft brown sugar
2 teaspoons	ground ginger
½ teaspoon	baking soda
6 tablespoons	margarine
2 tablespoons	honey
	nuts, seeds, currants,
	and/or glacé cherries

1. Sift together dry ingredients.
2. Melt together margarine and honey; add to dry ingredients.
3. Leave dough to cool. Cover and refrigerate for 1 hour.
4. Roll out on floured board.
5. Cut into gingerbread-man shapes with floured cutter and decorate with nuts, seeds, currants, and/or cherries.
6. Place on greased baking sheet leaving room to spread.
7. Bake at 350° for 12–15 minutes or until edges are lightly browned.
8. Leave to harden on sheet for 5 minutes before moving to wire rack to cool.
   Yield: 12.

Speculaas

This is a seasonal Dutch koekje *that Ria's family traditionally baked to celebrate the St. Nicholas festivities on December 6. But now we celebrate all the year round. The unique blending of the spices in this* koekje *makes it very special.*

1 cup	whole wheat flour
1 cup	all-purpose flour
⅔ cup	soft brown sugar
⅝ cup	unsalted butter
½ teaspoon	baking powder
¼ teaspoon	salt
2½ teaspoons	cinnamon
1½ teaspoons	mixed spice*
½ teaspoon	ground ginger
½ teaspoon	ground cloves
1 tablespoon	buttermilk or yogurt

1. Mix all ingredients in bowl until smooth and blended.
2. Shape into log 2″ in diameter.
3. Chill for half an hour.
4. Cut into ¼″ slices.
5. Bake on greased baking sheet at 325° for 15–20 minutes or until lightly browned and set.
6. Cool on wire rack.
   Yield: 20.

*If not available, substitute ½ teaspoon mace, ½ teaspoon coriander, ½ teaspoon cumin, ¼ teaspoon nutmeg.

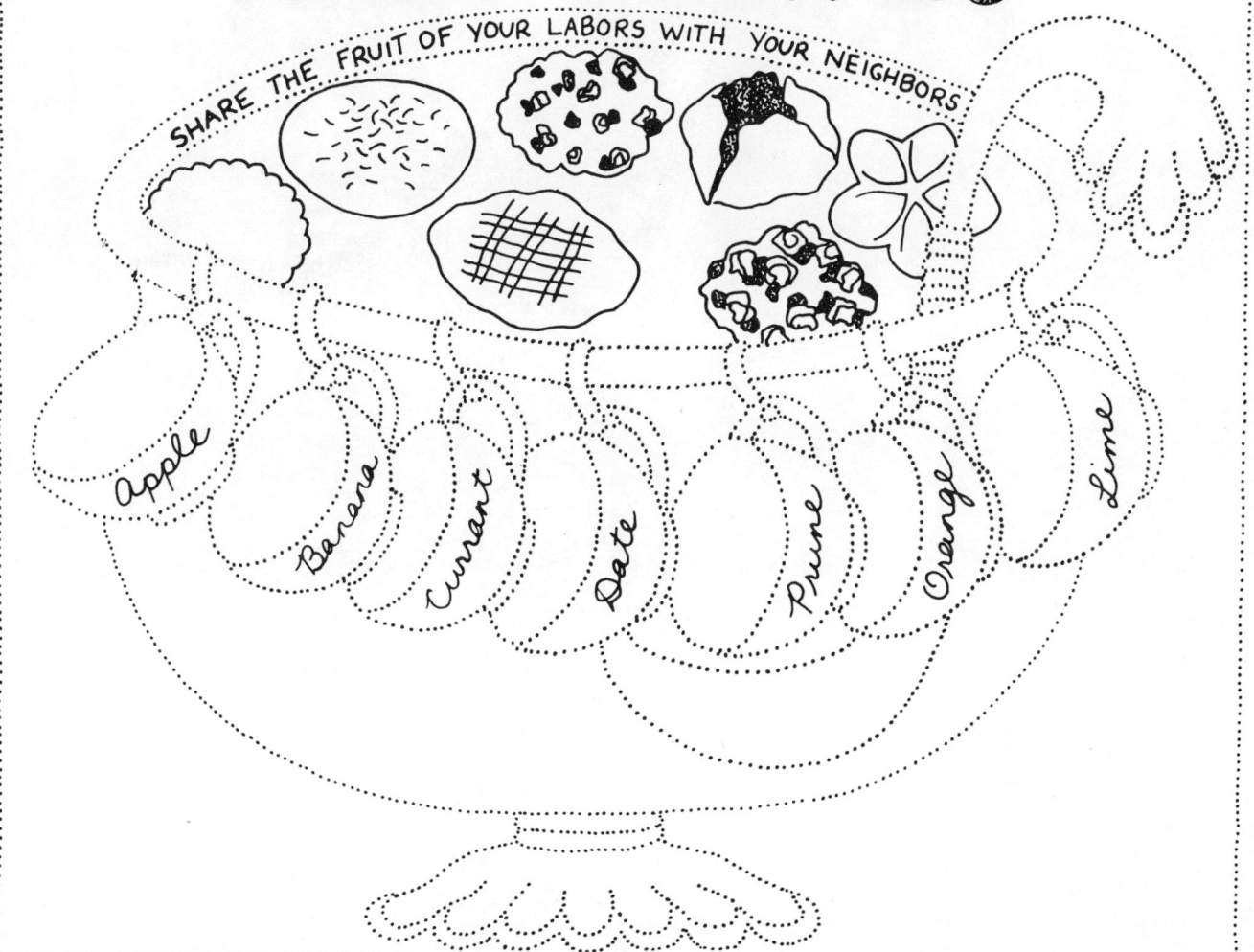

FRUIT COOKIES

SHARE THE FRUIT OF YOUR LABORS WITH YOUR NEIGHBORS

Apple Banana Currant Date Prune Orange Lime

Banana Cookies

These cookies are packed full of wholesome ingredients. Our children love them. They are soft, moist versions of an oatmeal cookie, naturally sweetened by the banana, and are at their best when warm, just out of the oven.

1½ cups	whole wheat flour
1 teaspoon	baking powder
¼ teaspoon	baking soda
1 teaspoon	cinnamon
¼ teaspoon	nutmeg
1 cup	raw sugar
½ cup	unsalted butter, softened
2	eggs
2	ripe mashed bananas
1½ cups	rolled oats
½ cup	chocolate chips
½ cup	chopped walnuts

1. Mix together flour, baking powder, soda, and spices.
2. Add sugar, butter, eggs, and bananas.
3. Beat until smooth.
4. Fold in oats, chocolate chips, and nuts.
5. Drop heaping teaspoonfuls onto greased baking sheet, allowing 2" for spreading.
6. Bake at 350° for 12 minutes.
7. Remove from pan and cool on wire rack.
   Yield: 36.

Currant Cookies

We guarantee these will always be your "currant" favorites! The lemon rind gives this cookie a light, tangy sweetness. Of course, raisins can easily be substituted for the currants, as can any other chopped dried fruit.

1 cup	unsalted butter
½ teaspoon	mace
1 teaspoon	vanilla extract
1 cup	raw sugar
1	egg
1 cup	all-purpose flour
1 cup	whole wheat flour
1 cup	currants
	grated rind of a large lemon

1. Cream together butter, mace, vanilla extract, and sugar.
2. Beat in egg.
3. Gradually add flours.
4. Stir in currants and lemon rind.
5. Wrap dough in foil or plastic wrap and refrigerate for 1 hour.
6. Roll out on lightly floured surface into 1" balls.
7. Place on greased baking sheet allowing 2" for spreading.
8. Press tops with fork dipped in sugar in crisscross pattern, flattening cookies slightly.
9. Bake at 350° for 12–15 minutes until lightly browned.
10. Remove from pans. Cool on wire rack.
    Yield: 40.

Date Cookies

These cookies are naughty but nice, just like Sandy, who introduced them to us. For those who want to be good *and nice, cut down on the sugar proportions, according to your own conscience.*

1 cup	unsalted butter
1⅓ cups	soft brown sugar
2	eggs
1 teaspoon	vanilla extract
1½ cups	whole wheat flour
1 teaspoon	baking soda
½ teaspoon	salt
3 cups	rolled oats
¾ cup	chocolate chips
1 cup	chopped dates

1. Beat together butter and sugar until light and fluffy.
2. Add eggs 1 at a time, beating well after each addition. Add vanilla extract.
3. Stir in flour, soda, and salt.
4. Add oats, chocolate chips, and dates. Mix well.
5. Drop by tablespoonfuls onto greased baking sheet, allowing 3″ for spreading.
6. Bake at 350° for 15–20 minutes, until lightly brown and firm.
7. Remove from pan and cool on wire rack.
   Yield: 40.

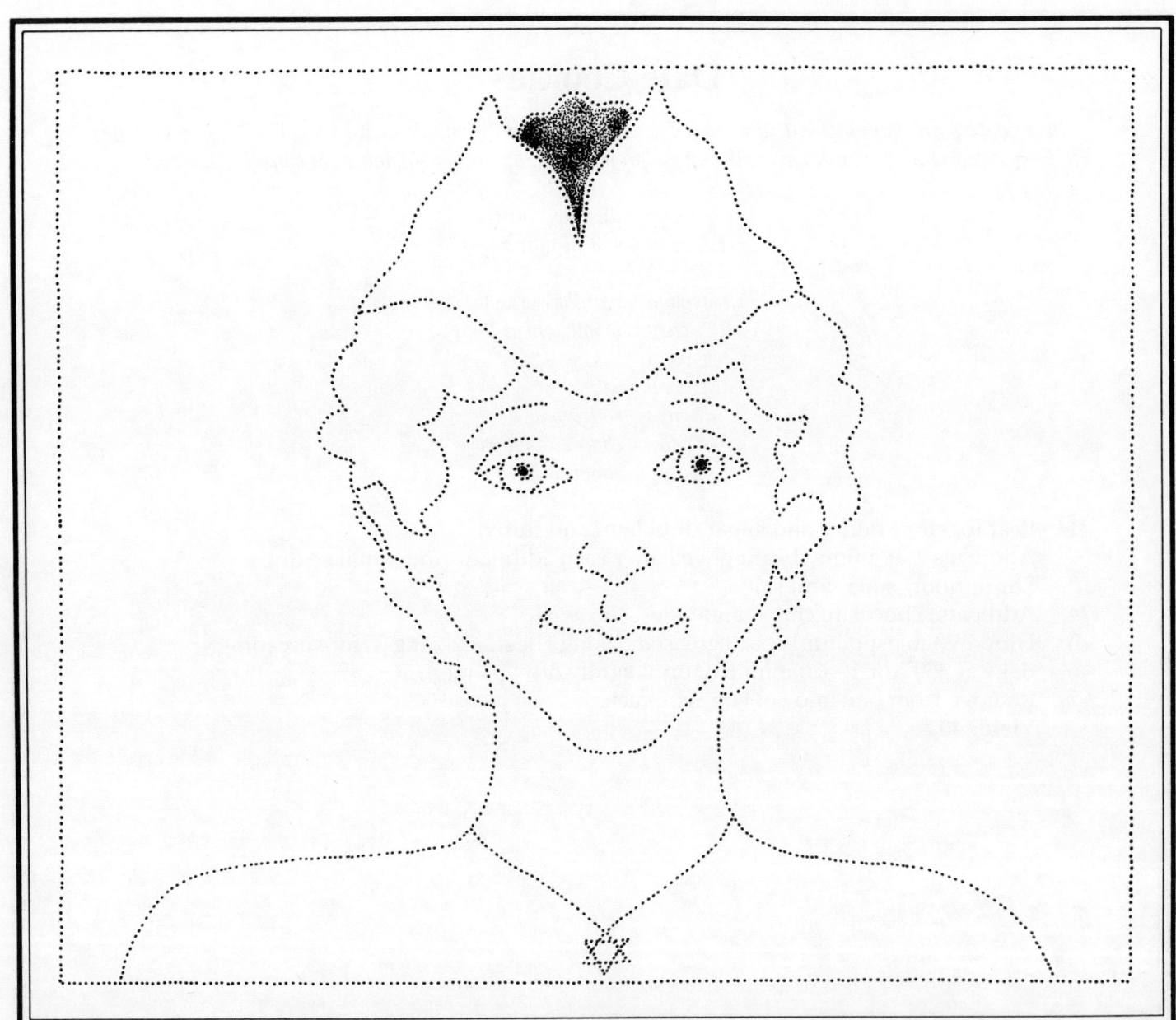

Hamantashen

These triangular cookies, baked by Jews during the traditional Purim festival, commemorate their victory over the tyrant Haman in the ancient kingdom of Persia. Hamantashen resemble the three-cornered hat that Haman wore. The sweet fruit filling and the rich flaky pastry will melt in your mouth.

Filling

1 cup	dates, pitted and chopped
1 cup	prunes, pitted and chopped
½ cup	raisins
2 tablespoons	orange juice
2 tablespoons	orange marmalade
1 tablespoon	honey
½ cup	chopped walnuts

Pastry

½ cup	cream cheese
½ cup	unsalted butter
1 cup	all-purpose flour
2 tablespoons	granulated sugar
1 tablespoon	grated orange rind
¼ teaspoon	salt
1	egg mixed with 1 teaspoon water

1. Place all filling ingredients in saucepan and simmer gently for about 30 minutes until thick and soft. Leave to cool.
2. Combine all pastry ingredients except egg and wrap and chill for at least 1 hour.
3. Roll pastry on floured surface to ¼″ thickness.
4. Cut into 3″ rounds. Brush with beaten egg wash.
5. Place 1 teaspoonful of filling on each round.
6. Pinch 3 corners together around filling to form triangles.
7. Place on lightly greased baking sheet.
8. Bake at 400° for about 15 minutes, until golden.
9. Remove from pan. Cool on wire rack.
   Yield: 20.

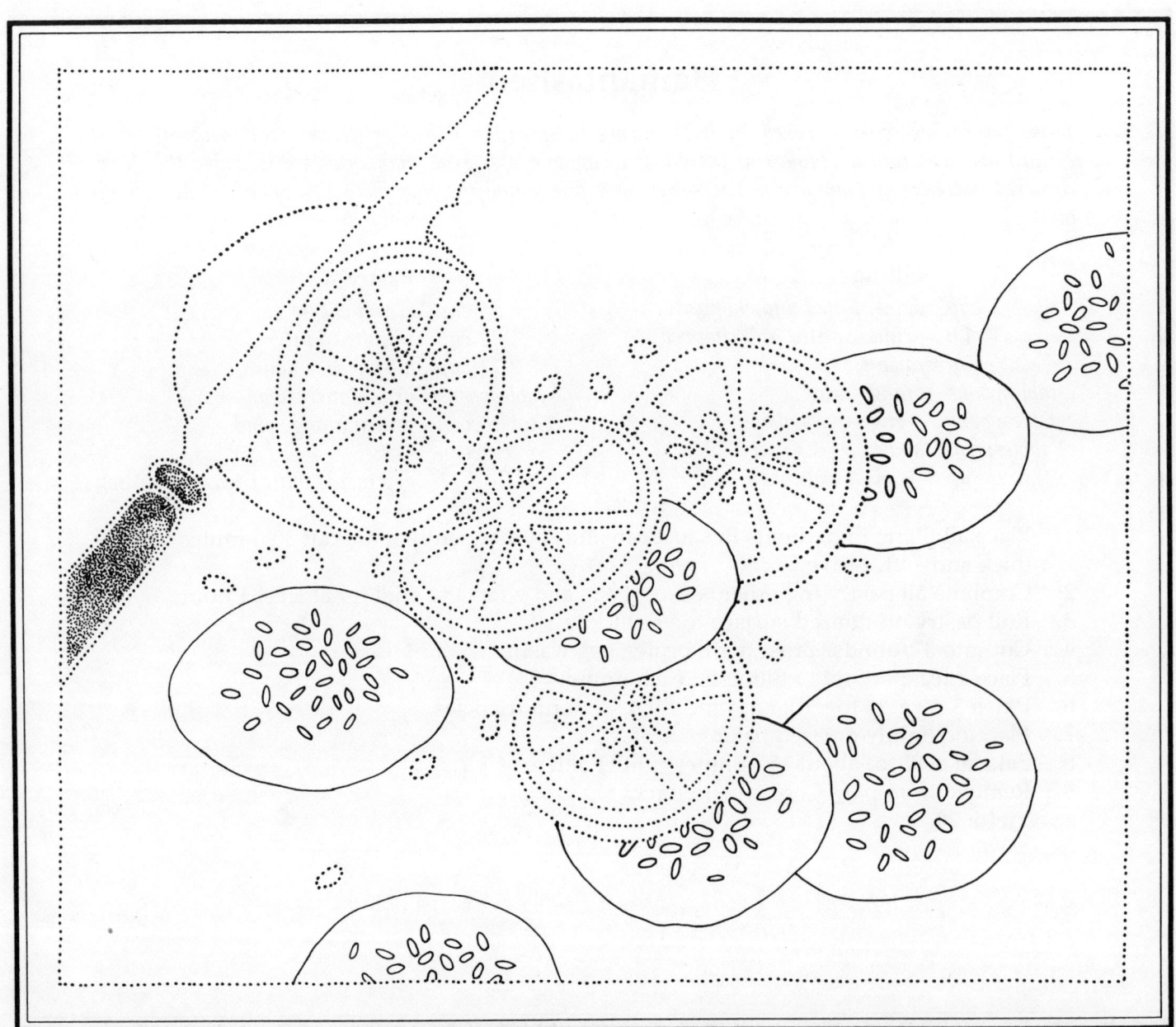

Orange Cookies

Refreshing as a glass of orange juice, full of zest and flavor.

1 cup	unsalted butter
1⅓ cups	raw sugar
1	egg
2 tablespoons	grated orange rind
2½ cups	whole wheat flour
1 teaspoon	baking soda
½ teaspoon	nutmeg
2 teaspoons	cinnamon
½ teaspoon	salt
1 cup	chopped almonds
4 tablespoons	orange juice
	chocolate sprinkles or
	chopped chocolate

1. Cream butter and sugar together.
2. Add lightly beaten egg and orange rind.
3. Sift together flour, baking soda, nutmeg, cinnamon, and salt, then add nuts.
4. Fold flour into butter mixture, alternating with orange juice.
5. Shape into 1" balls. Place on ungreased baking sheet, allowing 2" for spreading. Press down lightly with fork.
6. Top with chocolate sprinkles.
7. Bake at 350° for 20 minutes or until lightly browned and set.
8. Remove from pan. Cool on wire rack.
   Yield: 30.

Variation in preparation: Bake in logs as in mandelbread (allow at least five more minutes' baking time), cut into ¾" slices and leave in oven another couple of minutes without disturbing. Remove carefully from pan to cooling rack.

Lime Biscuits

This cookie is ideal for company. The exotic lime flavor adds distinction to the refined blend of flour and sugar.

$\frac{5}{8}$ cup   unsalted butter
$\frac{2}{3}$ cup   granulated sugar
2 cups   sifted cake flour
2   limes

1. Cream butter and sugar until light and fluffy.
2. Fold in sifted flour, along with rind and juice of 2 limes.
3. Knead lightly and roll into 1" balls.
4. Place on greased baking sheet. Press with floured cookie press to ¼" thick.
5. Bake at 350° for 20 minutes.
6. Remove from pan. Cool on wire rack.
   Yield: 32.

Applesauce Cookies

This is an excellent way of using leftover applesauce. But these cookies are so good that you won't need an excuse to bake them. The best result is obtained by using our own applesauce recipe (on page 124) or your own fresh homemade version. The thicker and spicier, the better.

1 cup	dark brown sugar
¾ cup	vegetable oil
1 teaspoon	vanilla extract
4 cups	rolled oats
1 cup	chopped walnuts
½ teaspoon	salt
1 cup	thick homemade applesauce

1. Beat together brown sugar and oil until well blended.
2. Add vanilla extract.
3. Mix in oats, walnuts, salt, and applesauce.
4. Drop heaping teaspoonfuls onto greased baking sheet.
5. Flatten the rounds with a floured glass.
6. Bake at 325° for 30 minutes.
7. Remove from pan. Cool on wire rack.
   Yield: 36.

Applesauce

8	large cooking apples,
	peeled, cored, and sliced
¼ cup	lemon juice
¼ cup	soft brown sugar
1 teaspoon	cinnamon
½ teaspoon	nutmeg
½ teaspoon	ground cloves
½ teaspoon	ground cardamom
¼ teaspoon	ground ginger

1. Place apples in large saucepan. Sprinkle with lemon juice; add sugar and spices.
2. Cook, covered, over low heat adding a little water if mixture is too dry.
3. When soft and pulpy, mash with potato masher or in blender.
4. If too runny at this stage, reduce liquid by boiling without lid until consistency thickens.
5. Remove pan from heat and leave to cool.
   Yield: 4 cups.

ABOUT THE AUTHORS

Diane Fine

Diane's love of cooking is probably related to her passion for art and dance, two lifelong outlets for her creativity.

 After graduating from Sir George Williams University in Montreal and the University of Toronto, majoring in fine arts, she began a career as a commercial illustrator and art teacher. An avid fitness buff, she has also studied dance and recently established a dancercise school in Toronto.

 Diane has studied cooking for many years in Toronto and England, while raising a family of three boys and baking sumptuous treats for her devoted husband.

Ria Teale

Ria was born in Beverwijk, Holland (the country where cookies originated), into a long line of professional bakers. From an early age she helped in the preparation of baked goods for her family's local bakery, gaining valuable firsthand experience.

 She now has her own family of two children and a husband to cook for and is continually experimenting in the professionally equipped kitchen at her home in Carlisle, England.

 Ria has introduced much of her traditional Dutch cooking to friends in the United Kingdom and is renowned in the community for her culinary talents and experience.